Fossil Ridge Public Library District
386 Kennedy Road
Braidwood, Illinois 60408

5/02

American Symbols
AND THEIR Meanings

THE
NATIONAL
ANTHEM

American Symbols
AND THEIR Meanings

THE
NATIONAL
ANTHEM

JOSEPH FERRY

MASON CREST PUBLISHERS
PHILADELPHIA

First printing

1 3 5 7 9 8 6 4 2

Library of Congress Cataloging-in-Publication Data
on file at the Library of Congress

ISBN 1-59084-033-X

Publisher's note: all quotations in this book come
from original sources, and contain the spelling and
grammatical inconsistencies of the original text.

American Symbols
AND THEIR **Meanings**

CONTENTS

Introduction

THE IMPORTANCE OF AMERICAN SYMBOLS

Symbols are not merely ornaments to admire—they also tell us stories. If you look at one of them closely, you may want to find out why it was made and what it truly means. If you ask people who live in the society in which the symbol exists, you will learn some things. But by studying the people who created that symbol and the reasons why they made it, you will understand the deepest meanings of that symbol.

The United States owes its identity to great events in history, and the most remarkable American Symbols are rooted in these events. The struggle for independence from Great Britain gave America the Declaration of Independence, the Liberty Bell, the American flag, and other images of freedom. The War of 1812 gave the young country a song dedicated to the flag, "The Star-Spangled Banner," which became our national anthem. Nature gave the country its national animal, the bald eagle. These symbols established the identity of the new nation, and set it apart from the nations of the Old World.

To be emotionally moving, a symbol must strike people with a sense of power and unity. But it often takes a long time for a new symbol to be accepted by all the people, especially if there are older symbols that have gradually lost popularity. For example, the image of Uncle Sam has replaced Brother Jonathan, an earlier representation of the national will, while the Statue of Liberty has replaced Columbia, a woman who represented liberty to Americans in the early 19th century. Since then, Uncle Sam and the Statue of Liberty have endured and have become cherished icons of America.

Of all the symbols, the Statue of Liberty has perhaps the most curious story, for unlike other symbols, Americans did not create her. She was created by the French, who then gave her to America. Hence, she represented not what Americans thought of their country but rather what the French thought of America. It was many years before Americans decided to accept this French goddess of Liberty as a symbol for the United States and its special role among the nations: to spread freedom and enlighten the world.

This series of books is valuable because it presents the story of each of America's great symbols in a freshly written way and will contribute to the students' knowledge and awareness of them. It is to be hoped that this information will awaken an abiding interest in American history, as well as in the meanings of American symbols.

—*Barry Moreno,*
librarian and historian
Ellis Island/Statue of Liberty National Monument

The guns of Fort McHenry overlook the Chesapeake Bay. A failed assault on this fort by British troops in 1814 inspired a lawyer named Francis Scott Key to write "The Star-Spangled Banner." His poem would eventually be set to music, and would become the national anthem of the United States.

BATTLE AT FORT McHENRY

As he watched from the deck of a ship anchored in the waters of Chesapeake Bay on a warm summer night in 1814, Francis Scott Key was deeply worried about the future of the United States.

Two years earlier, President James Madison had declared war on Great Britain, because British warships often stopped American ships. However, things did not go well for the United States in the early stages of the war. The American soldiers were poorly trained and badly under-supplied. They were no match for the British troops. By 1814, the British had marched into the nation's *capital* in Washington, D.C., and burned the

White House and other government buildings. This bold military move shook the young nation.

Key, a respected young lawyer, had been asked by friends to seek the release of a doctor who had been taken prisoner as the British troops left Washington and headed back to their ships at sea. With the blessing of President Madison, Key and another man boarded the British ship to *negotiate* with British officials on the doctor's behalf. After much discussion, Key succeeded in convincing the British to let his friend go free. But Key and the others were not allowed to leave the ship immediately. The British feared the men knew too much about the British plans to invade Baltimore, an important city in Maryland.

The first British target was Fort McHenry, which was far enough from the city to provide protection to the citizens of Baltimore and surrounded on three sides by water. This meant enemy ships sailing into Baltimore would have to pass the fort first. The British knew if they could take Fort McHenry, Baltimore itself would quickly fall and the young country would crumble.

For 25 hours, the British bombarded the fort with relentless force from dozens of ships anchored in the Chesapeake Bay. At times, it was difficult for Key to see the fort because of the thick smoke that filled the air. His eyes focused mainly on the huge *garrison* flag that flew above the fort. As long as the stars and stripes still flew, Key knew the fort had not fallen into enemy hands.

Finally, at daybreak, Key's weary eyes strained through the morning mist to see the fort. He couldn't tell if the flag that flew was the stars and stripes or the Union Jack. And then, at last able to see clearly in the gleam of the morning's first rays of sunshine, Key could see that although the American flag was tattered and singed from the battle, it was still waving proudly!

Relieved that the fort had withstood the vicious attack, Key pulled an envelope from his jacket pocket and began writing the words that eventually would become part of the *national anthem*: "'Tis the star-spangled banner—O long may it wave. O'er the land of the free and the home of the brave!"

No one knew it at the time, but Key's simple four-stanza poem would go on to become a battle cry for the nation. It would be sung

> The British fired 1,500 bombshells at Fort McHenry, including specialized Congreve rockets that left red tails of flame ("the rockets red glare") and bombs with burning fuses that were supposed to explode when they reached their target but often blew up in midair instead ("the bombs bursting in air").

before sporting events and at other important moments, in honor of the men and women who fought so bravely for freedom. It would provide inspiration and hope in troubled times. And it would serve as a reminder of the time when an overmatched fort stood up to a brutal attack from foreign invaders and won.

This etching shows Francis Scott Key as a young man. Key was born during the American Revolution and grew up in the early days of the United States. After years of study, he became a lawyer, practicing in Maryland and Washington, D.C.

YOUNG FRANCIS

*T*he author of the national anthem was born into a wealthy colonial family. In 1720, his great-grandfather Philip Key had traded the known comforts of life in England for the unfamiliar sights and sounds of the English colony of Maryland, where he became a successful lawyer. John Ross Key, Francis' father, fought in the American Revolution. He was also a judge and a farmer. At the time of his son's birth in 1779, he owned a 3,000-acre *plantation* in Frederick, Maryland known as Terra Rubra. The name of Francis Scott Key's first home means "red land" and refers to the rich red clay found in the ground of the plantation.

The Key plantation was spectacular. Surrounded by rolling fields, shaded woods, quiet streams, and breathtaking views of the distant Blue Ridge Mountains, it was an *idyllic* place to grow up during America's first few years of peaceful independence.

Because there were no schools near the plantation, Key and his sisters were educated at first by their parents. Their father taught them the history of the American Revolution and described all that he saw on his travels through the county as a judge. Their mother taught them to read and write and to appreciate the beauty of poetry. She also taught the slaves that lived and worked on the family's plantation to read and write and conducted prayer services for them. Young Francis attended these services and learned early in life to respect all people.

At age 10, Francis left Terra Rubra to attend school in Annapolis. He entered the new St. John's Grammar School there and lived with his grandmother's sister, who had a house near the campus.

When he arrived in the fall of 1789, Francis knew Annapolis was an important city in the history of the country. Congress had met in its State House, and George Washington used the same State House to give his farewell speech when he resigned his *commission* in the Continental Army.

As exciting as the atmosphere in the town was, young Key was not happy. He wrote of this period, "Sad was

As a young man Francis Scott Key was interested in the history of the American Revolution, which had been going on when he was born in 1779. This drawing, which was made from sketches and details by eyewitnesses, depicts the British Army firing on minutemen near Lexington, Massachusetts.

the parting [from Terra Rubra], sad the days, and dull the school and dull the plays."

Eventually, Francis did adjust to St. John's. He took daily classes in grammar, studied poetry, and made friends. He also learned Latin and Greek. Educators of the time believed true education did not begin until students knew these ancient languages.

At 14, Francis enrolled in the freshman class at St. John's College. Over the next three years he studied such varied subjects as algebra, trigonometry, *metaphysics*, navigation, and geography. He also read the works of

Annapolis, Maryland, was an important city in the early days of the United States. In this painting by the American artist John Trumbull, George Washington resigns as Commander-in-Chief of the Continental Army in the State House at Annapolis on December 23, 1783. Six years later, Francis Scott Key would attend school in Annapolis.

the ancient Greek philosophers Plato and Aristotle.

Francis graduated from St. John's with honors when he was 17. He was the class *valedictorian*. He would later become a lifelong supporter of the school he had once thought dull.

In 1802, when Francis was 23 years old, he married Mary Tayloe Lloyd. At first, Key practiced law in Frederick, Maryland. But when he joined his uncle's firm in Washington, D.C., Francis and Mary settled in nearby Georgetown, Maryland, a lovely, thriving tobacco port.

Georgetown was a far nicer place to raise a family than the new national city, which was little more than a dusty village with muddy roads when it rained.

Perhaps because his own experience at St. John's had been so positive, Key understood the importance of giving all children a good education. At 30, he joined the Lancaster Society, which ran a school in Georgetown specifically designed for children whose parents could not afford private school tuitions. Key believed citizens had to reach beyond the comforts of their own lives to help others. Some of the positions he took were popular; others were not. They all demonstrated his *conviction* that everyone must be socially responsible.

In 1812 President James Madison declared war on Great Britain. However, the War of 1812 did not go well for the Americans. In this engraving, British troops burn Washington, D.C., in the summer of 1814.

THE WAR OF 1812

hroughout Key's childhood and first years in Georgetown, the United States was at peace. It had been about two decades since the bloody Revolutionary War and the young nation was in the process of growing into a world power.

There were rumblings, however, that eventually led the new country into another *confrontation* with Great Britain. The British, at war with France since 1803, refused to allow *neutral* nations such as the United States to trade with France unless the British inspected the goods first. In *retaliation*, the French refused to accept any cargo that had been inspected by the British.

These inspections and subsequent *embargoes* severely limited the United States' ability to get its goods to the European markets.

In addition, as the fighting with France took its toll on their navy, the British began to take sailors off American ships to fight on British warships. The Americans protested, but the British said they were only taking back their own sailors who had *deserted*.

Eventually, the United States felt it had to act. On June 18, 1812, the government declared war on Great Britain. It was the result of a steady increase in tensions between the two countries in the three-plus decades since the U.S. declared independence from England. In addition to British mistreatment of American sailors, other issues were Britain's friendship with Native Americans as well as trade policies and taxes.

When the War of 1812 broke out, the United States already was a large country. There were 18 states—the original 13 plus five (Vermont, Kentucky, Tennessee, Ohio, and Louisiana had been added). The country also claimed ownership of several large territories, including land that now includes Mississippi and Alabama. The largest U.S. territory at the time was Missouri, which encompassed most of the land of the vast Louisiana Purchase. That land would eventually become the states of Arkansas, Missouri, Iowa, Nebraska, Kansas and South Dakota, as well as parts of Texas, Oklahoma, Colorado, and Wyoming. In 1812, the territories were

A Scene on the FRONTIERS as Practiced by the HUMANE BRITISH and their WORTHY ALLIES

Bring me the Scalps and the King our master will reward you —

Reward for Sixteen Scalps

*Arise Columbia's Sons and forward press,
Your country's wrongs call loudly for redress;
The Savage Indian with his Scalping knife,
Or Tomahawk may seek to take your life,*

*By bravery aw'd they'll in a dreadful Fright
Shrink back for Refuge to the Woods in Flight;
Their British leaders then will quickly shake,
And for those wrongs shall restitution make.*

In this political cartoon, a British officer presents a Native American hunter with a gun for every 16 American scalps he supplies. The warrior's knife and axe are engraved with the initials "GR," which stand for the King of England, George III. Many Americans were angry that the British had encouraged Native Americans to fight against the colonists during the Revolution. Continued attacks by Native American tribes helped bring on the War of 1812.

sparsely settled by Indians and whites.

Not everyone in the United States was anxious to take on the powerful British empire. In the Northeast, for example, where many people depended on trade, shipping, and fishing for their livelihood, the war was a terrible hardship. Ships sat at the docks and thousands of seamen lost their jobs. In the South and the West, farmers faced huge *surpluses* and declining prices because there was no overseas market for their products.

Few people in New England wanted war with Britain. They were furious over the loss of their livelihoods and opposed U.S. policies so strongly that they

James Madison was the fourth president of the United States. He was born in Port Conway, Virginia. After his education at the College of New Jersey (later named Princeton University), Madison returned to Virginia and in 1774 assumed the first of several positions in state government. In 1780 he began three years as a state delegate to Congress under the Articles of Confederation, where he advocated a stronger national government.

As a member of the Virginia House of Delegates from 1784 until 1786, he secured passage of Thomas Jefferson's landmark religious freedom bill. A primary mover behind the Constitutional Convention of 1787, Madison included many of his own ideas in the final document. He also was instrumental in adding the Bill of Rights. For these contributions, historians often call Madison, "father of the Constitution."

Madison served in the U.S. House of Representatives (1789–97) and then as President Jefferson's secretary of state (1801–09). He was elected president and served from 1809 until 1817. During his administration the War of 1812 broke out. It produced the burning of Washington and no real victory. Still, Madison left office with a considerable amount of popularity.

Madison spent the last years of his life on his estate in Montpelier, Virginia. He died in 1836.

often claimed to feel more British than American. Congressmen from New England argued that war with Britain would ruin the fragile U.S. economy. They insisted that the government settle its differences with Britain peacefully. Many threatened to abandon the Union if it came to war.

The dispute with Britain was not limited to shipping restrictions and confrontations at sea. The British increased their efforts to provide Native Americans with arms and to incite them to fight against American settlers pushing into the frontier. In 1810, the attacks *escalated* into full-scale war between whites and pro-British tribes, including the Shawnee and Potawatomi.

Pro-war representatives in Congress were outraged by the British-Indian alliance. Some remembered how the British and Native Americans had worked together during the Revolutionary War. They sensed the same kind of cooperation happening again.

A declaration of war against Britain became possible with the election of 1811. Voters in the West and South were frustrated by economic troubles and British-supported Indian attacks. They elected about 40 candidates who were in favor of war. This gave the pro-war *faction* a majority in Congress for the first time.

Led by Henry Clay of Kentucky, who was elected Speaker of the House of Representatives, the pro-war faction controlled several important committees, including foreign relations, military affairs, and the navy. Now,

During the first half of the 19th century, Henry Clay was one of the most powerful men in Congress. He urged President James Madison to go to war against Great Britain in 1812. Clay would remain a force in national politics until his death in 1850.

every British insult, no matter how small, was magnified and loudly denounced in Congress.

Clay and the others convinced President James Madison to demand the British drop their restrictions on American shipping. When there was no immediate response from England, many felt the time for war had come.

What the Americans did not know was that an embargo on British goods imposed by Madison had begun to work. Many British politicians argued that the country needed American trade and called for suspending the shipping restrictions. British Prime Minister Spencer Perceval, a supporter of maintaining the restrictions, was shot and killed by a madman on May 11, 1812.

With the government in chaos, Parliament agreed to suspend the restrictions on June 16.

But because news of these events was slow to cross the Atlantic Ocean, the report of the suspension did not reach the United States until it was too late. On June 18, just two days after the major obstacle to peace between the two nations was removed, the United States declared war on Britain.

Francis Scott Key gestures toward the American flag still flying over Fort McHenry. The flag that inspired the "Star-Spangled Banner" measured 30 feet by 42 feet, about one-quarter the size of a basketball court. The flag had 15 stars and 15 stripes. Each stripe was two feet wide, and each star was about two feet across.

BOMBS BURSTING IN AIR

The early years of the war were not easy for the United States. Soldiers were not trained well and many battles were lost. There were also those who questioned the wisdom of fighting against the British again. The New England merchants felt that if it had been difficult before, now it would be impossible to trade on the world market.

It was not until 1814, after England had defeated Napoleon, that the British would test the stubborn, determined U.S. forces in Baltimore. To attack the city successfully, the British first had to seize the key to the city's defense, Fort McHenry.

British troops entered Chesapeake Bay on August 19, 1814. Five days later they invaded and captured Washington. They set fire to the *Capitol* and the White House, and the flames were visible 40 miles away in Baltimore. A thunderstorm at dawn kept the fires from spreading. The next day more buildings were burned and again a thunderstorm dampened the fires. Having done their work, the British troops returned to their ships in and around the Chesapeake Bay.

On the way, a civilian American doctor named William Beanes, a much-loved town physician from Upper Marlboro, arrested three disorderly British soldiers. When word got back to British officials, they had Dr. Beanes arrested for interfering with their military. He was taken to their *flagship*, the H.M.S. *Tonnant*, which was anchored in the Chesapeake Bay.

Francis Scott Key had mixed feelings about the war, but when the British fleet entered Chesapeake Bay on August 19, 1814, he volunteered for the local *militia*. The war was in his backyard, and he wanted to help.

In the days following the attack on Washington, American forces prepared for an assault on Baltimore that they knew would come by both land and sea. Word soon circulated that the British had carried off Dr. Beanes. Fearing he would be hanged, the townsfolk asked Key to help. Because Dr. Beanes was a family friend, Key appealed to President James Madison, who sent him to John Skinner, the American agent in charge of prisoner exchanges. Together, they set out for the English fleet. Key hoped his skill as a lawyer would help him convince the British to let Dr. Beanes go free. On September 2, Key wrote to his mother, "I am going in the morning to Baltimore. . . . Old Doct. Beanes of Marlboro is taken prisoner by the enemy, who threaten to carry him off. . . . I hope to return in about eight or 10 days, though it is uncertain, as I do not know where to find the fleet."

John Skinner was born on Feb. 22, 1788 in Calvert County, Maryland. He was an agricultural writer and editor who spent his early years on the family plantation. Skinner became a lawyer at age 21.

Following the outbreak of the War of 1812, President James Madison made him a prisoner agent. He represented the Union in negotiations with the enemy whenever the government wanted to exchange prisoners of war.

Skinner was assigned to assist Francis Scott Key in securing the release of Dr. William Beanes, who had been taken prisoner by the British as they left Washington, D.C. Skinner was chosen by President Madison because he knew several officers in the British fleet, including General Robert Ross and Admiral Alexander Cochrane.

After the war, Skinner served as postmaster in Baltimore and later as third assistant postmaster general of the United States. In 1845, under President James K. Polk, he was removed from office for political reasons. Skinner died six years later when he fell at the post office in Baltimore.

On the morning of September 3, Key and Skinner set sail from Baltimore aboard a *sloop* flying a flag of truce approved by President Madison. On September 7, they found and boarded the *Tonnant* to confer with the leaders of the British land and sea forces, General Robert Ross and Admiral Alexander Cochrane.

At first, the two British officers refused to release Dr. Beanes. But Key and Skinner produced a pouch of letters written by wounded British prisoners praising the care they were receiving from the Americans, among them Dr. Beanes. Finally, Ross and Cochrane relented but

An Irishman remembered most for his taste for discipline and and his courage, Robert Ross could be boastful. When asked at breakfast on the morning of September 13, 1814, just hours before his planned attack on Baltimore, whether supper should be prepared for him at the same place, General Ross answered, "I will have supper in Baltimore or in hell." Another time, he confidently predicted, "I will make my winter headquarters in Baltimore and subjugate the whole coast."

In 1814, Ross was ordered "to effect a diversion on the coasts of the United States" to help the British army gathering in Canada for an attack. He landed his army of about 4,500 men at North Point, just outside Baltimore, at 3 A.M. on September 12. Five hours later, his troops began their march toward Baltimore, 14 miles away.

About halfway there, Ross' army encountered a force of 3,200 militia under the command of General John Strickler. Although the British won the skirmish that day, a sharpshooter killed Ross. His body was shipped back to England in a cask of rum.

would not release the three Americans immediately because they had seen and heard too much of the preparations for the attack on Baltimore. A smiling Admiral Cochrane said to Skinner, "You could hardly expect us to let you go on shore in advance of us." They were placed under guard and forced to wait out the battle on a sloop behind the British fleet. They were out of danger there, and had a good view of what was to come.

To capture Baltimore, the British knew they first had to take Fort McHenry, which guarded the ocean approach to the city. Carefully, they maneuvered 16 of their smaller ships up the Patapsco River and placed them in two half-circles around the fort. On September 13, the ships began their *bombardment*.

The flag that flew over Fort McHenry had been ordered in the summer of 1813, when a *marauding* British fleet had appeared in the Chesapeake Bay. Major

Alexander Cochrane replaced the elderly Admiral John Borlase as commander of the British fleet in North America just before the War of 1812 began. His orders were to "assist in inflicting that measure of retaliation which shall deter the enemy from a repetition of similar outrages."

Cochrane hated Americans, one of the most important qualities he brought to the job, although he had seen very little of them first-hand. Most of his career had been spent in the Mediterranean and West Indies, much of it in administrative work. He had done a stint in Parliament and had been governor of Guadeloupe.

George Armistead, commander of the fort, asked for a flag so big that "the British would have no trouble seeing it from a distance."

Two officers were sent to the Baltimore home of Mary Young Pickersgill, a "maker of colours," and ordered the flag. Mary and her 13-year-old daughter Caroline used 400 yards of top-quality wool *bunting*. They cut 15 stars that measured two feet from point to point. Eight red and seven white stripes, each two feet wide, were cut. Laying out the material on the floor of a brewery, the flag was sewn together. By August it was finished. It measured 30 feet by 42 feet.

At 7 A.M. on the morning of September 13, 1814, the British bombardment began. The large American flag flew over the fort as the attack continued for 25 hours. The British fired 1,500 bombshells that weighed as much as 220 pounds apiece and carried lighted fuses that would supposedly cause them to explode when it reached its target. But the fuses weren't very dependable and often blew up in midair. That evening the bombardment stopped, but in the early morning hours of September 14, the guns of the British fleet roared to life, lighting the rainy night sky with grotesque fireworks.

When the British opened fire on Fort McHenry, the cannons in the fort fired back, but their shots fell short. The British ships were anchored two miles offshore, out of the range of the fort's cannons. There was nothing the defenders could do but wait for the shelling to stop.

The British bombarded the fort all day and night. Windows in Baltimore shook. The air in the harbor was heavy with the smell of gunpowder. It was a terrible battle, and Key witnessed it all: the huge "bombs bursting in air" and the bright "rockets' red glare."

A widow who made her living in Baltimore as a seamstress, Mary Pickersgill did not hesitate when she was asked to sew a flag that would fly over Fort McHenry. The flag would have to be big enough so "the British devils can see it from far down in Chesapeake Bay," according to an American general, John Strickler.

Pickersgill was following in the footsteps of her mother, Rebecca Young, who had been asked by George Washington to make the first banner of the American Revolution, the "Grand Union Flag."

Together with her 13-year old daughter Caroline, her mother, and two nieces, Pickersgill got right to work. She found an empty malt house nearby where the huge flag could be laid out flat on the ground. They would need more than 400 yards of hand-woven bunting to make the flag. Each stitch had to be hand-sewn, each of the 15 stars set carefully on the field of blue. Under normal circumstances, such a flag would take months to make. But Mary Pickersgill was determined to make it in less than two weeks.

Working sometimes past midnight, her eyes red-rimmed from exhaustion and candle smoke, Mary Pickersgill labored on the project until it was finished.

Today, the home of Mary Pickersgill, now called the Star-Spangled Banner Flag House, stands at 844 East Pratt Street in Baltimore. The house and the adjacent 1812 War Military Museum are open to the public every day except Monday.

During the night the British landed troops, intending to storm the fort from the rear. Key and others heard the assault and listened to the eerie silence that followed. When dawn finally broke, they did not know if the attack had succeeded.

Key looked over at Fort McHenry. Because there was no wind, he could not tell whose flag was flying. Then a slight breeze unfurled the flag at the fort. It was the Stars and Stripes! Fifteen hundred shells had been fired at the fort during a 25-hour period, but miraculously, the Americans had withstood both the shelling and the assault by British troops.

Key was overjoyed. Quickly, he wrote down the beginnings of a poem. Being an amateur poet and having been so inspired by the scene, Key began to write on the back of an envelope he had in his pocket. While sailing back to Baltimore he composed more lines.

That day, the British withdrew their remaining troops and sailed for the open ocean. Without Fort McHenry, they could not take Baltimore. Without Baltimore, they could not establish a stronghold on American soil.

On December 24, 1814, a

The receipt given to Mary Pickersgill by the U.S. Army shows that she was paid $405.90 for making the Star-Spangled Banner and $168.54 for making a smaller flag. Notes on the reverse of the receipt by Major George Armistead, Fort McHenry's commander, indicate that he received both flags on August 19, 1813.

Since 1964, the flag that inspired the Star-Spangled Banner has been on display at the Smithsonian Institution's Museum of American History. However, the years have taken a toll on the flag. In 1994 museum curators realized that the flag was in bad shape. It was taken down in December 1998 and carefully cleaned. A three-year project to conserve the flag began in June 1999. Visitors to the Smithsonian can see the technicians carefully working to preserve the grand old flag.

little more than three months after the British bombardment of Fort McHenry, the Treaty of Ghent ended the war. One of the main reasons the United States had gone to war against Britain in the first place–the seizure of its ships and sailors–wasn't even mentioned in the settlement.

O say can you see ~~through~~ by the dawn's early light
What so proudly we hail'd at the twilight's last gleaming.
Whose broad stripes & bright stars through the perilous fight
O'er the ramparts we watch'd, were so gallantly streaming?
And the rocket's red glare, the bomb bursting in air,
Gave proof through the night that our flag was still there
O say does that star spangled banner yet wave
O'er the land of the free & the home of the brave?

On the shore dimly seen through the mists of the deep,
Where the foe's haughty host in dread silence reposes,
What is that which the breeze, o'er the towering steep,
As it fitfully blows half conceals half discloses?
Now it catches the gleam of the morning's first beam,
In full glory reflected now shines in the stream,
'Tis the star-spangled banner — O long may it wave
O'er the land of the free & the home of the brave!

And where is that band who so vauntingly swore,
That the havoc of war & the battle's confusion
A home & a Country should leave us no more?
~~Their b~~
Their blood has wash'd out their foul footsteps pollution
No refuge could save the hireling & slave
From the terror of flight or the gloom of the grave,
And the star-spangled banner in triumph doth wave
O'er the land of the free & the home of the brave.

O thus be it ever when freemen shall stand
Between their lov'd home & the war's desolation!
Blest with vict'ry & peace may the heav'n rescued land
Praise the power that hath made & preserv'd us a nation.
Then conquer we must when our cause it is just,
And this be our motto — "In God is our trust,"
And the star-spangled banner in triumph shall wave
O'er the land of the free & the home of the brave.

The copy of "The Star-Spangled Banner" that Key wrote in his hotel room remained in his family for 93 years. In 1907 it was sold to Henry Walters of Baltimore. In 1934, the Walters Art Gallery bought it at auction in New York from the Walters estate for $26,400. The Walters Gallery later sold the manuscript to the Maryland Historical Society for the same price.

THE NATIONAL ANTHEM

After returning to Baltimore the night after the bombardment of Fort McHenry, Key finished his poem and showed it to his brother-in-law, telling him he thought it should be set to the tune known as "To Anacreon in Heaven," a popular English drinking song. Key's brother-in-law took the poem to a printer, who distributed handbills throughout the city. Initially, the verses were published under the title "The Defence of Fort McHenry" and the author was listed simply as "a gentleman from Maryland."

Because printing of newspapers in Baltimore had been suspended from September 10 until September 20, the poem did not appear in the *Baltimore Patriot* until September 21. By October, newspapers around the country were printing the poem. It was also being sung in theaters and had been renamed "The Star-Spangled Banner" through popular usage. Key's song became a unifying cry to help the Americans fight the war. The battle for Baltimore might have been relegated to a military footnote in history if Key's words had not immortalized the courage of the soldiers at Fort McHenry.

By the 1850s, "The Star-Spangled Banner" was found in schoolbooks. Throughout the 19th century, "The Star-Spangled Banner" remained one of several popular patriotic songs. In 1916, by executive order, President Woodrow Wilson ordered it played at military events.

Its baseball *debut* was in 1918. League officials had considered canceling the World Series due to World War I, until they learned that American soldiers in France were looking forward to hearing about the games. At the seventh-inning stretch of the first game, the band suddenly began playing "The Star-Spangled Banner" as a patriotic gesture. Players and spectators stood, took off their hats, and sang. The song was repeated at subsequent games. During World War

Although there are four stanzas to "The Star-Spangled Banner," the other three are usually not sung out of respect to the British, who are now our friends and allies. The second and third stanzas contain negative comments about the British.

Military personnel unfurl a massive American flag during the singing of the National Anthem before Game 3 of the 1998 World Series between the San Diego Padres and the New York Yankees.

II, the tradition of singing or playing the anthem spread to other sporting events.

While "The Star-Spangled Banner" had been acknowledged as America's unofficial national anthem since at least 1914, it was not until 1931 that an Act of Congress, signed by President Herbert Hoover, made it official. The act read, "Be it enacted by the Senate and House of Representatives of the United States of American in congress assembled, That the composition consisting of the words and music known as "The Star-Spangled Banner" is designated as the National Anthem

The Star-Spangled Banner

Oh, say, can you see, by the dawn's early light,
What so proudly we hail'd at the twilight's last gleaming?
Whose broad stripes and bright stars, thro' the perilous fight,
O'er the ramparts we watch'd, were so gallantly streaming?
And the rockets' red glare, the bombs bursting in air,
Gave proof thro' the night that our flag was still there.
O say, does that star-spangled banner yet wave
O'er the land of the free and the home of the brave?

On the shore dimly seen thro' the mists of the deep,
Where the foe's haughty host in dread silence reposes,
What is that which the breeze, o'er the towering steep,
As it fitfully blows, now conceals, now discloses?
Now it catches the gleam of the morning's first beam,
In full glory reflected, now shines on the stream:
'T is the star-spangled banner: O, long may it wave
O'er the land of the free and the home of the brave!

And where is that band who so vauntingly swore
That the havoc of war and the battle's confusion
A home and a country should leave us no more?
Their blood has wiped out their foul footsteps' pollution.
No refuge could save the hireling and slave
From the terror of flight or the gloom of the grave:
And the star-spangled banner in triumph doth wave
O'er the land of the free and the home of the brave.

O, thus be it ever when freemen shall stand,
Between their lov'd homes and the war's desolation;
Blest with vict'ry and peace, may the heav'n-rescued land
Praise the Pow'r that hath made and preserv'd us as a nation!
Then conquer we must, when our cause it is just,
And this be our motto: "In God is our trust"
And the star-spangled banner forever shall wave
O'er the land of the free and the home of the brave!

In 1916 President Woodrow Wilson (left) ordered that the Star-Spangled Banner be played at military events. President Herbert Hoover (right) signed the act that officially made the song the national anthem of the United States in 1931.

of the United States of America."

The law does not include the words of the anthem. Because several different versions date back to Key's original, there is no definitive set of words. In the first verse, for example, the third line, "broad stripes and bright stars" was also written as "bright stars and broad stripes." In the same verse, the word "perilous" was also written as "clouds of the."

From that terrible night in 1814 through today, the song written by Francis Scott Key has been instilled in the hearts of each new generation of Americans. It is a symbol of the freedom that we enjoy in this country and the responsibility we have to help keep the rest of the world free from tyranny and oppression.

1779 Francis Scott Key is born.

1789 Key leaves his family's plantation, Terra Rubra, to attend school in Annapolis.

1793 Key enrolls in St. John's College.

1796 Key graduates from St. John's College.

1802 Key marries Mary Tayloe Lloyd.

1803 British and French begin war.

1806 Key takes over uncle's law practice.

1807 Key argues case before Supreme Court.

1812 United States declares war on England.

1814 Key volunteers for militia; British capture Washington on August 24, burning important buildings; bombardment of Fort McHenry begins on September 13; treaty signed between U.S. and Great Britain on December 24.

1843 Francis Scott Key dies on January 11.

1916 President Woodrow Wilson makes "The Star-Spangled Banner" the official song of the U.S. Armed Forces.

1931 An Act of Congress makes "The Star-Spangled Banner" the national anthem of the United States on March 3.

bombardment—an intensive and sustained attack by bombs or artillery fire.

bunting—heavy cloth or paper that is colored, often used for decoration.

capital—the city that serves as the official center of government for a state or nation.

Capitol—a building in Washington where Congress passes laws and conducts other business.

commission—an appointment to the rank of officer in the armed forces.

confrontation—an encounter of two sides with opposing opinions or policies.

conviction—firmness of belief or opinion.

debut—the first public presentation of a performer, program, or performance.

desert—to leave a military post without permission, never intending to go back.

embargo—an order from the government prohibiting the movement of merchant vessels from or into its ports.

escalate—to increase or make something larger than it was before.

faction—a group within a larger group whose opinions do not always agree with the majority.

flagship—a ship bearing the flag officer or the commander of a fleet.

garrison—a body of troops stationed at a fortified place such as a fort.

idyllic—charmingly simplistic or poetic; a pleasant scene.

marauding—the act of randomly carrying out violent acts.

metaphysics—a branch of philosophy that studies that nature of existence.

militia—a body of men called out periodically for military drills but serving as full-time soldiers only in emergencies.

national anthem—the official song of a country or nation.

negotiate—to discuss a dispute with the intention of working out a settlement acceptable to both sides.

neutral—taking neither one side nor the other in a dispute.

plantation—a farm or estate with crops that are tended by resident laborers.

retaliation—the attempt to gain revenge against an enemy or foe.

sloop—a single-masted sailing vessel.

surplus—an extra amount that is left over after all needs have been filled.

valedictorian—the student who graduates with the best academic record.

FURTHER READING

Adams, John Winthrop. *Stars and Stripes Forever: The History of Our Flag*. New York: Smithmark Publishers, Inc., 1992.

Ferry, Joseph. *The American Flag*. Philadelphia: Mason Crest Publishers, 2003.

Gray, Susan. *The American Flag*. Minneapolis: Compass Point Books, 2001.

Kroll, Steven. *By the Dawn's Early Light: The Story of the Star-Spangled Banner*. New York: Scholastic, 1993.

Mandrell, Louise. *Sunrise Over the Harbor*. Fort Worth, Texas: Summit Group, 1993.

Patterson, Lillie. *Francis Scott Key: Poet and Patriot*. New York: Chelsea Juniors, 1991.

Sedeen, Margaret. *Star-Spangled Banner: Our Nation and Its Flag*. Washington, D.C.: National Geographic Society, 1993.

INTERNET RESOURCES

Information about Francis Scott Key

http://www.flagday.com/history/francis_scott_key.shtml
http://www.theshop.net/slworley/fckey.html

The battle of Fort McHenry

http://www.bcpl.net/~etowner/battle.html

The Star-Spangled Banner

http://www.150.si.edu/chap3/flag.htm
http://www.flaghouse.com
http://americanhistory.si.edu/ssb/2_home/fs2.html

History of the American Flag

http://www.usflag.org
http://www.icss.com/usflag/toc.html